S

THE ULTIMATE GUIDE ON HOW TO MAKE SLIME RECIPES

Table of Contents

Introduction

Kids simply love to play with Slime. And I was one of those kids. I watched everything I could find on YouTube and refined my technique until I could make slime on an industrial scale! My allowance went on ingredients and I was selling my slimy creations for a $2 a squishy handful. **Find my homemade slimes below.**

Make sure you follow some of my top slimy tips as well. And whatever you do – don't eat it! Slime will make you sick – how do I know this? Because my 15-year-old big sister tried to eat some of my green glitter slime! That's teenagers for you I suppose.

Also slime is made from glue – it might say washable on the label but trust me this is very misleading. How do I know this? Because my friend dropped my red glitter slime on our sofa and the sofa still has red glitter pretty much permanently stuck to it – **That's why You need to be extra careful when handling slime.**

Note: If you prefer not to use **<u>Borax</u> you can easily substitute it with any of the following... liquid laundry detergent, contact lens solution or shaving cream.**

Chapter1: Fundamentals of slime

What Is Slime?

Slime (also called Flubber) has been a staple of kid's lives since the late 1970's when it became a kids's toy. Slime is a gooey and sticky substance that is somewhere on the spectrum between a solid and a liquid and its viscosity (the speed which a liquid can flow) can actually vary depending on temperature. But just what is this fun substance?

The beginning of this play dough in fluid gel consistency dates back to 1970's. Slime game pulp produced by an American toy company has become a legend in many different years. Slime doughs, which are sold in many countries in the 90s, are now becoming a great play activity for kids at home.

It can exist in nature, interestingly enough, and is used as a defense mechanism. Slime is also prevalent in humans, especially come cold and flu season in the form of snot. There is, however, one animal that shows off its slime. That animal is the beautiful Hagfish (pictured below). As you can see in the picture below, Hagfish secrete slime as a defense mechanism against other fish (and sometimes humans). This slime coats everything, and in water, it is extremely effective in stopping or slowing down any predators. The Hagfish slime is so effective, in fact, that our United States military is looking into creating a synthetic slime to be used on our aircraft carriers and other marine ships to be used to protect our ships.

Now synthetic slime, on the other hand, is slightly different (and far less nasty) than the Hagfish slime. Besides being a great toy, it can actually be used to help save people. Slime can be used to plug wounds, and can even be used as armor for divers.

Important notes about slime
Do not give to children with highly sensitive skin conditions.

Never leave young children alone with slime.

There are some recipes that require Borax to make slime but some kids have sensitive skin so in such cases you should chose slime recipes that use liquid starch.

Never pour it down the drain. The slime could block your drains.

It is strongly recommended that you always wash your dishes by hand rather than using your dishwasher. Some of the ingredients especially the bubble bath might not be good to put in the dishwasher.

Don't eat slime or put it in your mouth.

Wash your hands thoroughly after you have finished playing with slime.

What is the science of slime?

The main ingredients in slime are glue and boric acid (we will cover this later on) react to each other to create this fascinating thing. The glue has molecules in it that slide around easily actually link up with the boric acid molecules that slowdown that sliding. That slowed down flow makes the liquid become considerably more viscous and turns it into an almost solid object. Now there are recipes for slime that exclude some ingredients, but this is the general idea behind slime.

Slime is not the only non-Newtonian fluid you are probably familiar with. Some examples of non-Newtonian liquids are:

Ketchup

Mustard

Silly putty

Caramel

Slime top tips

Keep it in an airtight container. Otherwise it dries out and skins over.

Slime loves to be played with so the more you handle it the better it becomes.

If you are going to make this, a lot of mess is going to be involved. So ask first.

Borax – this isn't easy to get hold of sometimes. I prefer to use it, and I bought a box on Amazon. You don't need much and the box will last ages, and it's not too expensive.

Try checking out discount stores for ingredients. I find that I can get huge bottles of glue for just a dollar, and discount It is a solution which is used for cleaning, rinsing, disinfecting and storing your slime. -elaborate more on this explain

Save old jars with lids to keep your creations in.

Everything you read about slime refers to "washable school glue." Just a heads up guys & girls this is a lie – it doesn't wash out and the end of my mom's sofa is permanently covered in "washable school glue." So you have been warned.

Food coloring – this is great for slime. I mean who wants just boring clear or white slime. But be warned you might end up with green hands, and yes I have had to go to school with one green hand and one blue one after it didn't wash off completely.

Borax tip – get an adult to boil a kettle before you want to make slime. The Borax will not dissolve properly in cold water, and it won't work properly.so make your Borax solution in advance and let it cool down.

Contact Solution – you need to find the contact eye solution that has boric acid in it. I use Optrex which does have the boric acid in it.

Chapter 2: How to make Gold Slime

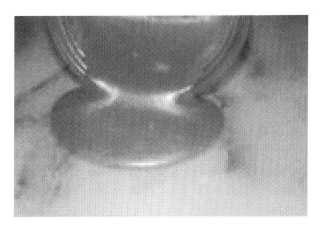

Blast off to a galaxy far far away with this galactic slime! For extra fun add some small plastic glow in the dark stars that you can buy in craft stores. This recipe calls for dye, not food coloring. Be careful, if you get dye on your clothes it will stain them.

Ingredients

- Bowl
- Spoon
- Liquid starch
- Clear, tacky glue

- Silver or gold glitter -A few drops of dye (a mixture black, purple, and dark blue look best)

Directions

1. Pour 1 cup of glue into bowl -Add a few drops of dye into bowl -Add glitter and stir
2. Add ⅓ cup of liquid starch and stir. It will be very goopy
3. Keep stirring until it becomes a ball. Take the ball out and knead it. There you have it!

Chapter3: How to make Glow in the dark

There is a glow in the dark slime recipe in the first How to Make Slime and Other Revolting Recipes. This recipe is a bit different, and uses paint instead of glue. It also is more "see through" slime because it calls for clear glue instead of white glue.

Materials

- 2 Bowls
- Stirring Utensil -Water
- Liquid starch
- Elmer's Glue
- Glow in the Dark Paint

Directions

1. In the first container, pour ½ cup of liquid starch
2. In the second container, mix ½ cup of glow in the dark glue (you can also add a bit of glow in the dark craft paint to white glue if you can't find light in the dark blue) and ½ cup of water
3. Mix container one and two and stir lightly (not thoroughly).
4. Let the mixture sit for at least five minutes.
5. After five minutes, stir the mixture thoroughly, and let sit for an additional five minutes.
6. Pick up your creation! Enjoy stretching and molding

Chapter4: How to make a fluffy Super Smooth Slime

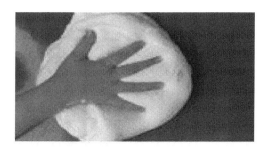

This recipe is a little different because it includes some kids shampoo in the method. This gives the slime a sleeker and springier texture and also it smells great. Another plus is you are going to get to play with shaving cream again!

Ingredients

- Shaving cream - 2 tbs
- Any kids shampoo – a complete one that includes conditioner is best – 2 tbs
- One teaspoon of salt
- Liquid corn starch

Directions

1. First of all, put shampoo into a mixing bowl. If you are not sure how much the shampoo be used then start with little quantity. Try at least two tablespoons

initially. You can always add more later to make a larger batch.

2. The trick with this recipe is to keep the shampoo and the shaving cream in equal quantiles. I recommend making small amount first so you can judge the quantities before scaling up.

3. Add liquid corn starch until you get a smooth, creamy mixture.

4. Salt – the quantity to add is one teaspoon for every two tablespoons of shampoo. So as you increase the amount of shampoo you also increase the amount of salt.

5. To get this slime to work once it has been mixed thoroughly put the bowl in the freezer and cool it for around 15 mins. When you take it out of the fridge the slimy magic will have happened, and it will be ready to play with.

Chapter5: How to Make Jelly Slime

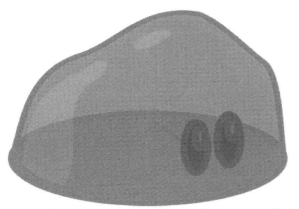

https://pixabay.com/en/slime-jelly-aspic-jello-blue-148995/

This is a great way to make slime. The recipe uses either jelly crystals or jelly cubes. These give your slime an extra boost as it will smell of whatever flavor jelly you used. Just remember - **don't eat it – no matter how beautiful it looks**

Ingredients

- One bottle of clear school glue
- One bottle of water
- Half tbs of borax
- Half a cup of hot water
- Two tbs of jelly crystals or two jelly cubes - any flavor

Directions

1. Pour all the glue into a bowl. Then fill the bottle with warm water and give it a shake. This will make sure you are getting all of the adhesive from the bottle. Pour the water into the bowl

2. Get a wooden spoon and give a right mix, don't put your hands in yet the mixture is too sticky now.

3. Fill a cup with warm water and add in your jelly cubes or crystals and stir it with a spoon until the jelly has dissolved completely.

4. Add to the dissolved jelly mixture half tbs of Borax and keep stirring until the Borax has evaporated as well.

5. Slowly add the jelly/Borax solution to your glue and stir with a spoon. Very soon it will start to form into slime. Get your hands in for the final mixing.

Chapter 6: How to make Magnetic slime

This is a fun homemade paint. I think you'll really like it! It is one of the most fun experiments ever for kids. BUT you must use magnet for this or it won't work.

Ingredients

- ¾ cup flour
- Food coloring
- ½ cup water
- Bowls
- Spoons
- baking soda
- coffee filter

- vinegar

Directions

1. In a bowl mix flour and water
2. Add 2-3 drops of food coloring
3. Keep mixing until smooth
4. That's it! Make a masterpiece!

Chapter 7: How to make Glitter Slime

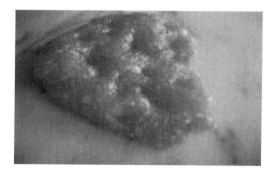

Glitter slime is awesome. A great way to do this is to get a pack of various colors of glitter from a craft shop. When you have made your slime divide it up and add ¼ of a teaspoon of colored glitter to each of the portions of slime. It doesn't matter later if they get all mixed up into one substantial glittery gloopy slime ball either.

Ingredients

Ingredient you need are:

- Bottle of school glue
- 1 Cup of water
- One teaspoon borax
- One teaspoon water

Directions

1. Add the Borax to a cup of water and stir until the Borax has dissolved.
2. Squeeze the glue into a bowl and add one teaspoon of water and mix using a wooden spoon.
3. A little at a time add the Borax mixture into the bowl, keep stirring as you add it in.
4. Once your slime starts to form get your hands in and mix it until you get it to the right slimy consistency.
5. Divide your slime up and add in different colored glitters.

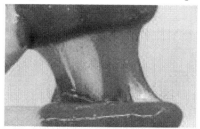

For extra fun with your ectoplasm, find a printed newspaper. If you press the ectoplasm slime on the words, it makes a copy! Have fun stretching it out!

Ingredients:

- One bottle of school white glue
- 1 ½ cups water
- White glitter. The bigger and chunkier glitter the cooler this will look
- Two bowls
- Two teaspoons Borax
- pigment
- food coloring

Directions

1. Mix glue and water in a bowl.
2. Add your white glitter.
3. In a SEPARATE glass bowl mix the Borax into a cup of warm water.
4. Mix the two bowls and stir

Borax can be hard to get hold of in some places, and so here is my "borax-cheat" recipe if you can't get your hands on the box.

Most of the Slime recipes used in the home use borax, but it is luckily possible to make slime even without using borax. In this recipe, we will learn that how a Slime is prepared without using borax. Makes 2 cups are enough for one kid

Ingredients

- 4 ounce bottles washable school glue

- One to two drops of liquid food coloring
- A handful of Glitter
- 2 to 3 tablespoons saline solution
- One teaspoon Baking Soda
- Measuring Spoons
- Mixing Spoon
- A mixing bowl or a big plastic
- A screw top jar or container with an airtight lid
- Now we look at the Color the Glue

instructions:

1. Put the glue into a medium bowl. The glue comes out slowly. It can be worth running the bottles under the hot tap for a moment, and this makes the paste pour out quicker. Blend in the food coloring and glitter if you are using some.
2. Don't put too much color in or you'll dye your hands, and also it is extra liquid, so it will make your slime soggy.
3. Don't worry if your slime seems a bit lumpy adding the baking soda at the next step will sort this out.
4. Adding the Baking Soda
5. Baking soda is the next ingredient to add and once this has been stirred in your

mixture will start to become a lot
smoother.

6. Contact Lens Solution
7. Put 2 tbsp. of contact lens solution into
   the bowl and continue to stir your
   mixture. The mixture should start to
   harden and become rubbery. If not the
   slimy magic has not happened so keep on
   mixing.
8. Mix all the ingredients
9. As you mix it, you will see the
   consistency start to change and the slime
   will begin to form.
10. Mix the slime with your hands
11. This is the best moment – you get to
    plunge your hands into the brand new
    never touched before slime Pick up the
    slime and work between your two hands
    so that it becomes smooth. If the slime is
    still too "slimy" and sticking to you,
    work in another half tablespoon of
    contact lens solution as required.
12. It's Slime Time!
13. As soon as it is all mixed and your slime
    consistency is right, it's SLIME TIME.
    The slime is ready to play with, and I
    don't know anyone who wouldn't want to
    play with their slimy creation straight
    away.

This is a super soft play slime. The best part? You only need three ingredients and it is a clear, transparent, fun slime that you can see through! All slime recipes should be made with parental permission and supervision, but especially this one as it involves boiling water.

Ingredients

- Lux flakes or other pure soap flakes.
- Hot water

- Food coloring (unless you want to leave it white) -A large container

Directions

1. Add 1 cup of soap flakes to 3 cups of hot or boiling water. Mix with a whisk or electric beaters.
2. Add food coloring -Let your slime rest overnight. It will thicken up.
3. There you go!

Blast off to a silver far away with this shiny slime! For extra fun add some silver stars that you can buy in craft stores. This recipe calls for borax, not food coloring. Be careful, if you get dye on your clothes it will stain them.

Ingredients:

- One bottle of school white glue -1 ½ cups water
- Pearly dry pigment. You will need to go to a craft or hobby store for this ingredient

- One bowl
- Glass bowl
- Two tsp Borax

Directions

1. Mix glue and water in a bowl.
2. In a SEPARATE glass bowl mix the Borax into a cup of warm water.
3. Add ¼ cup of the pearlescent pigment in the color of your choice
4. Mix the two bowls and stir!
5. A blob will form, take it out and knead the blob (knead-means to rub and squish over and over) -Enjoy your slime!

Conclusion

Many slime recipes exist, which can help you to create a slime with any attribute you wish for. Whether you want to magnetize it, light it up or make it look like mucus, you will find the perfect slime for you. You can add food coloring, confetti, and even sand into your slime mixture to totally change up the consistency of your slime.

Heck, you can even add shaving cream to make super fluffy slime that is fun to play with.

If you, or your child, have any skin allergies then you will want to stay away from boric acid. Borax is not in itself dangerous, but it is something to keep a eye on. You can find boric acid not only in some contact solution but in cleaning products as well. If you are in a pinch, then you can make slime in so many different ways you are sure to find a recipe for stuff you already have laying around the house. **You can use contact lens solution containing boric acid when combined with baking soda and glue instead of borax.**

If you can't find what you want, this book is a great place for anything you will need to make your slime.

Note: If you prefer not to use **<u>Borax</u> you can easily substitute it with any of the following... liquid laundry detergent, contact lens solution or shaving cream.**

12374740R00020

Made in the USA
San Bernardino, CA
10 December 2018